FOOTBALL STARS UP CLOSE

J.J. Watt

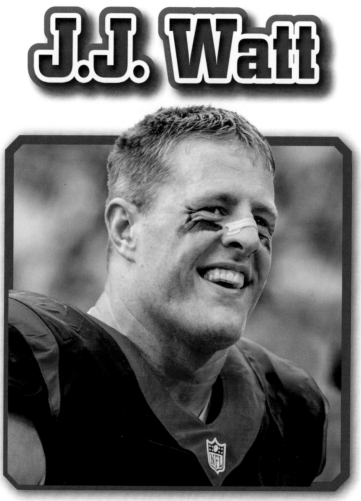

By K.C. Kelley

Consultant: Craig Ellenport
Former Senior Editor, NFL.com

BEARPORT
PUBLISHING

New York, New York

Credits

Cover and Title Page, © Trask Smith/Zuma Press/Newscom; 4, © Erik Williams/Cal Sport Media/Newscom; 5, © Trask Smith/Zuma Press/Newscom; 6, © Rudy Hardy/Cal Sport Media/Newscom; 7, © Rudy Hardy/Cal Sport Media/Newscom; 8, © Mike de Sisti/MCT/Newscom; 9, © David Stluka; 10, © Jamie Roach/Shutterstock; 11, © Dwane Lindsey; 12, © Alan Schwartz/Cal Sport Media/Newscom; 13, © Benny Sieu/MCT/Newscom; 14, © AP Photo/Bill Baptist; 15, © Mike McGinnis/MCT/Newscom; 16, © AP Photo/Bill Baptist; 17, © Trask Smith/Zuma Press/Newscom; 18, © Art Foxall/UPI/Newscom; 19, © George Bridges/MCT/Newscom; 20, © Andrew Richardson/Icon SMI CBV/Newscom; 21, © AP Photo/Aaron M. Sprecher; 22, © Trask Smith/Zuma Press/Newscom.

Publisher: Kenn Goin
Editor: Jessica Rudolph
Creative Director: Spencer Brinker
Photo Researcher: Shoreline Publishing Group LLC
Layout Design: Patty Kelley

Library of Congress Cataloging-in-Publication Data

Names: Kelley, K. C., author.
Title: J.J. Watt / by K.C. Kelley.
Description: New York : Bearport Publishing Company, Inc., [2016] | Series:
    Football Stars Up Close | Includes bibliographical references, webography
    and index. | Audience: Ages: 7–12._
Identifiers: LCCN 2015039374| ISBN 9781943553372 (library binding) | ISBN
    1943553378 (library binding)
Subjects: LCSH: Watt, J. J., 1989——Juvenile literature. | Football
    players–United States—Biography—Juvenile literature.
Classification: LCC GV939.W362 K45 2016 | DDC 796.332092–dc23
LC record available at http://lccn.loc.gov/2015039374

For more information, write to Bearport Publishing Company, Inc., 45 West 21st Street, Suite 3B, New York, New York 10010. Printed in the United States of America.

10 9 8 7 6 5 4 3 2 1

Contents

Defense and Offense

Most fans agree that J.J. Watt is great on **defense**. They love the way the **NFL** player storms over blockers to knock down passes and **sack** quarterbacks. In 2014, J.J.'s fans discovered something else he could do—play **offense** and score touchdowns!

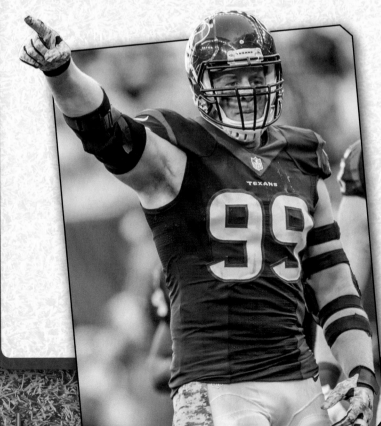

J.J. plays for the Houston Texans.

In his first three seasons in the NFL, J.J. made 74 tackles in which yards were lost for the opposing teams. That was the most tackles for loss in the NFL during those years.

In a game against the Tennessee Titans on November 30, 2014, J.J. did it all. In the fourth quarter, he sacked quarterback Zach Mettenberger, forcing him to **fumble**. Then J.J. **recovered** the ball himself. Later, Houston coaches put J.J. in on offense. After the snap, J.J. ran into the end zone and caught a pass thrown by Texans quarterback Ryan Fitzpatrick. Touchdown!

J.J.'s touchdown helped the Texans beat the Titans 45–21.

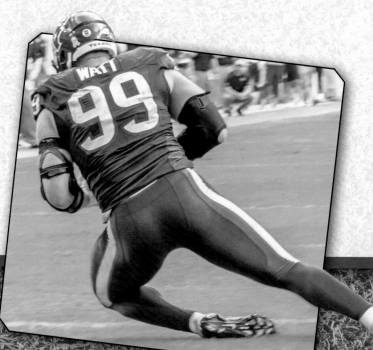

In the 2014 season, J.J. caught a total of three touchdown passes. He also scored on a fumble return and an **interception** return. He was the first NFL player in 66 years to score three times on offense and twice on defense in a season!

Football-Loving Kid

Justin James "J.J." Watt was born on March 22, 1989, in Waukesha, Wisconsin. He grew up with two younger brothers, Derek and T.J. They loved playing sports, especially football. The boys played the game in their backyard whenever they could. Young J.J. had a big dream—to one day play in the NFL.

J.J.'s brother Derek grew up to play football for the University of Wisconsin.

As a kid, J.J. also loved ice hockey. He was so good that he played in a youth tournament in Germany!

J.J. still enjoys playing hockey.

A New Position

In high school, J.J. joined the football team. He looked up to the team's quarterback, so J.J. wanted to play that position. He practiced and practiced, but only became the **backup** quarterback.

As a junior, J.J. tried a new position—**defensive end**. Suddenly, he was a star! His height and strength made him great at tackling players. J.J. was fast, too. This allowed him to also play **tight end**, catching passes and scoring touchdowns.

J.J. played on his high school's track and field team as well. He still holds his school's record in the shot put. Athletes need great strength to throw a heavy iron ball in this event.

A shot-putter

A Big Change

After high school, J.J. earned a **scholarship** to play tight end at Central Michigan University. However, he wanted to play for a stronger team. So, he **transferred** to the University of Wisconsin. Since Wisconsin had not offered him a scholarship, J.J.'s parents helped him pay for his first year there. He also paid for school with a job delivering pizzas. With his great playing on the field, J.J. soon earned a scholarship to Wisconsin!

When J.J. transferred from Central Michigan to Wisconsin, he changed positions from tight end to defensive end.

Central Michigan University's football team is called the Chippewas.

J.J. blocks a pass for the University of Wisconsin team, the Badgers.

College Star

J.J. played two full seasons with the Badgers. As a senior, he led the **Big Ten** with seven sacks. That year, he was awarded the Ronnie Lott Trophy as the best college defensive player.

J.J.'s next stop—he hoped—would be the pros. On April 28, 2011, the Houston Texans selected him in the first round of the **draft**. The former pizza delivery guy was in the NFL!

Wade Phillips, the former Texans' coach, called J.J. "the perfect player." The coach felt J.J. had the skills, size, and focus needed to be an NFL star.

J.J. at the draft

WATT 99

J.J.'s Badgers teammates congratulate him after he makes a tackle.

Rookie Success

As a **rookie**, J.J. helped the Texans make the **playoffs** for the first time in team history. In a playoff game against the Cincinnati Bengals, he returned an interception for his first NFL touchdown.

By the end of his second season, J.J. was one of the best players in the NFL. He led the league with 20.5 sacks. He even helped Houston make the playoffs again!

J.J. makes an interception against the Bengals during his rookie season.

How can a player earn half (0.5) a sack? When two players tackle a quarterback at the same time, each player earns half the sack.

J.J. sacks Miami Dolphins quarterback Ryan Tannehill.

Hard to Stop

After making the playoffs in 2011 and 2012, the Texans had a poor 2013 season. J.J. did the best he could, but his **stats** were down from earlier years. Part of the reason was that opponents tried to avoid him! Quarterbacks on other teams threw passes far away from J.J. so he couldn't knock balls down or intercept them. In some plays, teams used two or three players to block J.J. because he's so strong.

After the 2013 season, J.J. played in the Pro Bowl. That's the NFL's annual all-star game, which is played right after the regular season. J.J. has competed in three Pro Bowls.

J.J. (#99) is 6 feet 5 inches (196 cm) and 289 pounds (131 kg)!

What's Next?

The 2014 season turned out to be J.J.'s best year yet. On defense, he scored two touchdowns. He also knocked down ten passes. On offense, he caught three touchdowns. During the season, J.J. signed a contract to stay with Houston for several more years. Who knows what else this amazing player can do?

J.J. won't let anything get in the way of sacking a quarterback—even if it means ending up with a bloody nose!

J.J. won two NFL Defensive Player of the Year Awards, in 2012 and 2014.

J.J. became a YouTube star in 2014. From a standing position, he jumped on top of a stack of boxes that was 5 feet 1 inch (1.5 m) high! Video of his leap was seen by millions of people.

J.J.'s Life and Career

★ **March 22, 1989** — Justin James "J.J." Watt is born in Waukesha, Wisconsin.

★ **2003** — As a child, J.J. plays in several all-star hockey tournaments, including one in Germany.

★ **2007** — J.J. plays tight end for Central Michigan University.

★ **2009** — At the University of Wisconsin, J.J. plays defensive end for two years.

★ **2011** — The Houston Texans select J.J. in the NFL Draft.

★ **2012** — In Houston's first-ever playoff game, J.J. scores on an interception return.

★ **2012** — J.J. is named the NFL Defensive Player of the Year.

★ **2014** — J.J.'s five touchdowns are the most by a defensive player in 66 years.

★ **2014** — J.J. earns his second NFL Defensive Player of the Year Award.

Glossary

backup (BAK-up) a player who is ready to replace a starting player

Big Ten (BIG TEN) a group of universities that have formed an athletic league

defense (DEE-fenss) the part of a football team that tries to stop the other team from scoring

defensive end (dee-FEN-siv END) a player who tackles ball carriers

draft (DRAFT) an annual event in which NFL teams choose college players

fumble (FUM-buhl) to drop a ball or lose it to an opponent

interception (in-tur-SEP-shuhn) a pass that is caught by a defensive player

NFL (EN-EFF-ELL) letters standing for the *National Football League*, which includes 32 teams

offense (AW-fenss) the part of a football team that does most of the scoring

playoffs (PLAY-awfss) games played after the regular season that determine which two teams will compete in the Super Bowl

recovered (rih-KUV-urd) gained possession of a ball after it was dropped or lost by the opposing team

rookie (RUK-ee) a player in his or her first year of a pro sport

sack (SAK) when a defensive player tackles the quarterback

scholarship (SKAH-lur-ship) money given to a student to pay for school fees

stats (STATS) short for *statistics*; the numbers sports teams use to keep track of what players do on the field

tight end (TYTE END) a player on the offense who catches passes and blocks for other players

transferred (TRANS-furd) left one school to attend another school

Index

Bibliography

Ganguli, Tania. "J.J. Watt Scores Fifth TD of Season." www.ESPN.com (December 1, 2014).

Official Site of the Houston Texans: www.houstontexans.com

Official Site of the NFL: www.nfl.com

Read More

Fishman, Jon. M. *J.J. Watt (Amazing Athletes)*. Minneapolis, MN: Lerner (2014).

Frisch, Nate. *The Story of the Houston Texans (NFL Today)*. Mankato, MN: Creative Education (2014).

Scheff, Matt. *J.J. Watt (Football's Greatest Stars)*. Minneapolis, MN: ABDO (2016).

Learn More Online

To learn more about J.J. Watt, visit
www.bearportpublishing.com/FootballStarsUpClose